AI Therapy, Coaching & Behavioral Change

How AI Rewires Habits, Addiction & Self-Control

By Joe Correa

Published by Live Stronger Faster

This book is for educational and informational purposes only. The author and publisher are not engaged in rendering legal, financial, or other professional advice. Readers should consult a qualified professional before making any financial decisions.

First Edition

Table of Contents

Introduction

For centuries, human behavior has been viewed as stubbornly resistant to change. Habits were considered hardwired, addictions seen as moral failures or lifelong struggles, and self-control framed as a limited resource that only a disciplined few could master. Traditional therapy models, while helpful for many, often relied on slow, retrospective analysis and generalized frameworks that struggled to adapt to the complexity and individuality of the human brain. Today, that narrative is changing. We are entering an era in which artificial intelligence is transforming how behavioral change, therapy, and coaching are understood, delivered, and sustained—by working directly with the brain's natural capacity for neuroplasticity. This book explores that transformation in depth, revealing how AI-powered systems are reshaping habits, dissolving addictive loops, and strengthening self-regulation at a neurological level.

At its core, behavior is not a matter of willpower—it is a pattern encoded in neural circuits. Every habit, craving, emotional reaction, and impulse is the result of repeated electrical and chemical signaling across networks of neurons that have been reinforced over time. The brain is not static; it is constantly rewiring itself in response to feedback, reward, stress, and environment. What AI introduces into this process is precision. Unlike traditional approaches that depend on self-reporting, memory recall, or broad behavioral models, AI systems can continuously analyze patterns in thought, emotion, language, physiology, and decision-making. This allows for interventions that are not only personalized, but dynamically adaptive—responding in real time to the brain's changing state.

AI-driven therapy and coaching represent a fundamental shift from episodic support to continuous cognitive guidance. Instead of a once-a-week session or a generic program, individuals can now engage with intelligent systems that monitor behavioral signals throughout daily life. Language patterns in journaling, speech cadence, micro-pauses in writing, sleep metrics, heart rate variability, and even facial expressions can be used to detect emotional dysregulation, cognitive fatigue, or the onset of compulsive behavior. These systems do not replace human therapists; rather, they extend therapeutic insight into moments where change actually happens—during decisions, urges, and stress responses that occur outside the therapy room.

One of the most powerful applications of AI in behavioral change is habit rewiring. Habits are formed through repetition and reward, governed largely by the basal ganglia and reinforced by dopamine-driven learning loops. Breaking a habit requires more than suppression; it requires replacement—new neural pathways that offer equal or greater reward. AI excels at identifying the precise triggers, timing, and emotional states that activate a habit loop. By recognizing these patterns, AI systems can introduce targeted interventions at the exact moment a habit is likely to fire, offering alternative behaviors, reframed thoughts, or micro-rewards that gradually weaken the old circuitry while strengthening new ones. Over time, the brain reorganizes itself, not through force, but through guided adaptation.

Addiction, long misunderstood as a lack of character or discipline, is increasingly recognized as a maladaptive learning process embedded in neural reward systems. Substances, behaviors, and digital stimuli can hijack dopamine signaling, creating cycles of craving and relief that overpower rational decision-making. AI-based therapeutic models approach addiction not as a binary condition, but as a spectrum of neural reinforcement patterns. By analyzing behavior longitudinally, AI can detect subtle escalations, emotional precursors, and environmental cues that precede relapse—often before the individual consciously recognizes them. This predictive capability allows for early intervention, personalized coping strategies, and adaptive recovery plans that evolve alongside the brain's healing process. Behavioral coaching powered by AI also redefines accountability and motivation. Traditional coaching relies heavily on external reinforcement and self-discipline, which can fluctuate under stress or fatigue. AI systems, however, can provide consistent, nonjudgmental feedback grounded in data rather than emotion. They track progress objectively, highlight small wins that might otherwise go unnoticed, and adjust goals based on cognitive load and emotional resilience. This creates a feedback loop that mirrors how the brain learns best: through timely reinforcement, clarity, and manageable challenge. Over time, users begin to internalize these patterns, strengthening executive function and self-control networks in the prefrontal cortex.

Emotional regulation is another cornerstone of behavioral change, and one where AI demonstrates remarkable potential. Emotional reactions often occur faster than conscious thought, driven by limbic system activation. AI systems trained on emotional markers can detect early signs of dysregulation—such as language shifts, pacing changes, or physiological stress responses—and intervene with grounding techniques, cognitive reframing, or calming protocols. These interventions are not generic; they are tailored to the individual's emotional profile, trauma history, and cognitive style. With repeated use, the brain learns to regulate itself more efficiently, reducing reactivity and increasing psychological flexibility. This book also addresses the ethical and psychological considerations of AI-based therapy and coaching. As AI systems become more integrated into mental health and behavioral guidance, questions arise around privacy, dependency, autonomy, and trust. Effective AI therapy must empower individuals rather than replace agency. The goal is not to outsource decision-making, but to enhance awareness, insight, and self-mastery. When designed responsibly, AI serves as a mirror—reflecting patterns the brain cannot easily see on its own—and as a guide, offering tools that support long-term behavioral resilience rather than short-term compliance.

Importantly, AI-driven behavioral change is not limited to clinical populations. High performers, entrepreneurs, athletes, creatives, and professionals are increasingly using AI coaching systems to optimize focus, reduce procrastination, manage stress, and align daily behavior with long-term goals. In these contexts, AI acts as a cognitive amplifier—helping individuals identify friction points, eliminate self-sabotaging patterns, and build habits that compound over time. Behavioral excellence, once the domain of elite coaching and years of trial and error, is becoming more accessible, measurable, and sustainable.

Throughout this book, you will explore how AI therapy and coaching systems are designed, how they interact with the brain's learning mechanisms, and how they are applied in real-world scenarios—from addiction recovery and emotional healing to productivity and personal transformation. You will learn why behavioral change fails when it ignores neurobiology, and how AI succeeds by aligning with it. You will also gain insight into the future of behavioral science, where intelligent systems collaborate with human cognition to create lasting change at scale.

AI is not rewriting who we are—it is revealing how change has always worked beneath the surface. By making the invisible visible and the unconscious measurable, AI gives us unprecedented access to the mechanics of behavior itself. In doing so, it offers a new path forward: one where habits are redesigned rather than resisted, addiction is treated with precision rather than stigma, and self-control becomes a trainable neural skill rather than a fixed trait. This book invites you into that future, where therapy, coaching, and behavioral change evolve from hopeful intention into intelligent, adaptive transformation.

Chapter 1

The Neuroscience of Behavioral Change in the Age of Artificial Intelligence

Behavioral change has long been treated as a psychological challenge, but modern neuroscience reveals it is fundamentally a neurological process governed by adaptive circuitry in the brain. Every behavior—whether productive or destructive—is encoded through repeated neural firing patterns shaped by reward, emotion, stress, and reinforcement. These patterns are not abstract ideas; they are physical networks strengthened or weakened by experience. Artificial intelligence enters this domain not as a motivational tool, but as a system capable of observing, modeling, and influencing these neural dynamics with unprecedented precision. To understand how AI reshapes therapy, coaching, and self-control, one must first understand how the brain learns to behave in the first place.

The brain is a prediction machine. It constantly anticipates outcomes based on prior experience and adjusts behavior to minimize discomfort and maximize reward. Habits form when predictions are repeatedly confirmed. A behavior followed by relief, pleasure, or emotional regulation becomes encoded as efficient and reliable. Over time, the brain automates these behaviors to conserve energy, shifting control from conscious decision-making regions in the prefrontal cortex to subcortical structures responsible for automatic execution. This efficiency is evolutionarily advantageous, but it becomes problematic when the learned behavior is misaligned with long-term well-being. Addiction, procrastination, emotional reactivity, and compulsive behaviors all emerge from this same optimization process.

Traditional therapy models attempt to interrupt these patterns through insight, reflection, and conscious reframing. While valuable, these approaches often struggle because they operate at a slower cognitive layer than the behavior itself. Neural loops driving habits can activate in milliseconds, long before rational thought intervenes. Artificial intelligence changes this dynamic by operating at the same speed and scale as neural signaling patterns. By continuously analyzing behavioral data, AI systems learn how an individual's brain responds to stress, reward, anticipation, and failure. This allows interventions to be delivered at the precise moment when neural plasticity is most accessible.

Neuroplasticity is not evenly distributed across time. The brain is more receptive to change during moments of emotional activation, novelty, discomfort, or decision-making. AI systems excel at detecting these windows. Through analysis of language patterns, physiological signals, timing behavior, and contextual cues, AI can infer when the brain is entering a state of heightened learning potential. Rather than relying on generalized strategies, AI-driven therapy adapts to the individual's neurocognitive state in real time. This transforms behavioral change from a delayed, reflective process into an active, guided experience embedded within daily life.

Self-control, often misunderstood as a moral virtue, is better understood as a neurological skill rooted in executive function networks. These networks are finite and vulnerable to fatigue, stress, and emotional overload. When depleted, the brain defaults to previously reinforced habits regardless of intention. AI-based coaching systems recognize these fluctuations and adjust expectations accordingly. Instead of pushing rigid discipline, they modulate challenge levels, reduce cognitive load, and reinforce progress strategically. This trains the brain to associate regulation with success rather than exhaustion, gradually strengthening neural pathways responsible for impulse control and goal alignment.

Addictive behaviors represent an extreme case of maladaptive neuroplasticity. Dopamine-driven reward circuits become hypersensitized, while regulatory circuits weaken through disuse. AI systems approach addiction by mapping these imbalances rather than moralizing them. By identifying triggers, escalation patterns, and emotional precursors, AI can predict high-risk moments and intervene before relapse occurs. Over time, repeated AI-guided interventions retrain reward circuitry to respond to healthier stimuli, allowing the brain to recover its natural balance. This reframes recovery as neural rehabilitation rather than personal failure.

Behavioral change also depends heavily on identity reinforcement. The brain resists behaviors that conflict with self-concept and reinforces those that align with perceived identity. AI coaching systems incorporate this by tracking language shifts, belief patterns, and narrative framing. When individuals begin to see themselves as disciplined, resilient, or capable, corresponding neural patterns stabilize. AI accelerates this process by reflecting progress objectively, reinforcing identity-consistent behaviors, and minimizing cognitive distortions that undermine confidence. This creates a virtuous cycle in which behavior, belief, and neural structure evolve together.

What distinguishes AI-driven behavioral change from previous methodologies is its capacity for scale, personalization, and consistency. Human therapists and coaches are limited by time, memory, and emotional bandwidth. AI systems, by contrast, provide continuous observation without judgment or fatigue. They remember every data point, adapt instantly, and refine their models continuously. This does not diminish the value of human connection; instead, it enhances it by allowing therapy and coaching to focus on deeper relational and interpretive work while AI handles pattern recognition and real-time intervention.

As AI becomes more integrated into therapeutic frameworks, behavioral change shifts from episodic effort to continuous optimization. The brain learns not through occasional insight, but through repeated exposure to aligned feedback. AI supplies that feedback consistently, turning daily life into a training environment for neural growth. This chapter establishes the foundation for understanding how AI interacts with the brain's learning mechanisms, setting the stage for deeper exploration of habit formation, addiction recovery, emotional regulation, and long-term self-mastery in the chapters that follow.

The Pattern Beneath the Choice

Daniel had always believed his problem was discipline. He told himself this every morning when he reached for his phone before getting out of bed, every evening when he promised that tomorrow he would stop scrolling, stop snacking, stop postponing the life he intended to build. He read books, listened to podcasts, and even attended therapy sessions where he articulated his goals clearly and intelligently. Yet the behaviors remained stubbornly intact, resurfacing under stress as if they were immune to logic. What Daniel did not realize was that his brain was not resisting change—it was protecting efficiency.

When Daniel enrolled in an AI-powered behavioral coaching program, he expected reminders and accountability notifications. Instead, the system began by observing. It tracked his sleep patterns, his writing tone in daily reflections, the timing of his decisions, and the subtle emotional shifts that preceded his habitual behaviors. Within weeks, it identified patterns Daniel had never noticed. His most compulsive behaviors occurred not when he was tired, but when he felt cognitively overloaded. The brain, seeking relief, defaulted to familiar reward loops that provided immediate comfort.

One evening, as Daniel sat at his desk feeling the familiar pull toward distraction, the AI intervened—not with a command, but with a reframing question delivered at precisely the right moment. It asked him to delay the behavior by sixty seconds and offered a brief grounding exercise calibrated to his stress profile. The urge weakened. The brain, deprived of its expected reward, hesitated. In that hesitation, a new neural pathway began to form.

Over the following weeks, these interventions accumulated.

The AI adjusted its timing, tone, and strategies based on Daniel's responses. It learned when to challenge him and when to support him. Gradually, his sense of effort shifted. Behaviors that once required force became easier. The brain, recognizing new reward contingencies, began to favor the healthier patterns. Daniel noticed something unexpected—he no longer felt like he was fighting himself.

Months later, Daniel reflected on the change. He had not become more disciplined through willpower. He had become more aligned through design. The AI had not controlled him; it had revealed the mechanics beneath his choices. By guiding his brain through repeated, well-timed adaptations, it allowed him to rebuild behavior from the inside out. For the first time, change felt natural rather than forced—a quiet recalibration rather than a daily battle.

Daniel understood then that behavior was never the enemy. It was information. And with the right intelligence—both human and artificial—the brain could learn new patterns without resistance, rewriting not just habits, but identity itself.

Chapter 2

How AI Identifies, Interrupts, and Rewrites Habit Loops

Habits are not behaviors in isolation; they are closed-loop neurological systems designed for efficiency. The brain forms habits by linking a cue to an action and reinforcing that action with a reward, creating a self-sustaining circuit that runs with minimal conscious oversight. These loops operate beneath awareness, often activating before deliberate thought has time to intervene. Traditional behavioral change methods frequently fail because they attempt to suppress the action without fully understanding or addressing the cue and reward that sustain the loop. Artificial intelligence transforms this landscape by making habit loops visible, measurable, and modifiable at a granular level.

At the neurological level, habit loops are encoded primarily in the basal ganglia, which favors repetition and predictability. Once a loop is established, the prefrontal cortex gradually disengages, allowing the behavior to run automatically. This automation conserves cognitive energy but also makes habits resistant to change. AI systems excel at pattern recognition across large volumes of data, enabling them to detect the subtle cues that trigger habits—time of day, emotional state, cognitive load, environmental context, and even linguistic tone. By aggregating these signals, AI constructs a behavioral map that reveals not just what a person does, but why the brain initiates the behavior.

Interrupting a habit loop requires precision timing. If an intervention occurs too early, the brain ignores it; too late, and the behavior has already executed. AI-driven systems are uniquely suited to this challenge because they operate continuously and adaptively. As they learn an individual's behavioral rhythms, they identify the narrow windows where neural plasticity is most accessible. Interventions delivered during these moments do not rely on force or suppression; instead, they gently disrupt the expected sequence, creating a pause that weakens the loop's predictability. Over time, repeated disruptions erode the loop's efficiency, making it less automatic and more susceptible to change.

Rewriting a habit is not about elimination but substitution. The brain resists voids; when a habit is removed without replacement, it often resurfaces or mutates. AI systems facilitate habit replacement by testing alternative behaviors that satisfy the same neurological need for reward or regulation. These alternatives are not imposed uniformly. AI evaluates which substitutions generate comparable dopamine responses, emotional relief, or cognitive clarity for the individual. Through iterative feedback, the system refines these replacements until the brain begins to favor the new pathway over the old one.

Feedback is essential to reinforcement learning, and AI delivers feedback with a consistency and neutrality that human systems cannot match. Every successful interruption or substitution is logged, analyzed, and reinforced. The brain learns not through abstract motivation, but through immediate cause-and-effect associations. AI accelerates this learning by providing timely validation that strengthens emerging neural pathways. Even small behavioral shifts are amplified through feedback loops that encourage repetition, allowing new habits to stabilize more quickly than through traditional trial-and-error methods.

Crucially, AI recognizes that habit strength fluctuates. Stress, fatigue, emotional volatility, and cognitive overload all weaken regulatory circuits and increase reliance on automatic behavior. Rather than interpreting lapses as failures, AI models them as data points. When a habit reasserts itself, the system analyzes the conditions that enabled it, adjusting future interventions accordingly. This reframes relapse not as regression, but as information that improves the accuracy of the behavioral model. Over time, the system becomes more adept at predicting vulnerability and reinforcing resilience.

Habit loops are also deeply intertwined with identity. The brain reinforces behaviors that align with self-concept and resists those that conflict with it. AI coaching systems integrate identity reinforcement by tracking narrative language, belief statements, and self-referential patterns. As new habits form, the system mirrors these changes back to the individual, reinforcing the perception of growth and consistency. This alignment between behavior and identity strengthens long-term retention, ensuring that habits persist even in the absence of external prompts.

The ultimate power of AI-driven habit change lies in scalability and personalization. No two brains form habits in exactly the same way. AI systems continuously refine their understanding of each individual, allowing interventions to evolve alongside the brain's adaptation. This creates a dynamic partnership between human cognition and artificial intelligence—one where habits are not fought, but redesigned. In mastering habit loops, AI lays the foundation for deeper behavioral transformation, enabling lasting change rooted in neural architecture rather than fleeting motivation.

The Pause That Changed Everything

Sophia had tried to quit countless times. The habit wasn't dramatic or destructive enough to alarm anyone else, but it quietly eroded her confidence. Whenever she felt overwhelmed, she retreated into the same pattern—an automatic escape that left her feeling numb and frustrated afterward. She knew the trigger intellectually. She had discussed it in therapy. Yet knowing had never been enough. The habit always arrived faster than her awareness, like a reflex she could not outrun.

When Sophia began working with an AI behavioral system, she was skeptical. She assumed it would offer reminders or motivational messages, things she had learned to ignore. Instead, the system asked permission to observe. For weeks, it tracked her routines, emotional check-ins, and decision timing. It noticed patterns Sophia hadn't consciously registered—how the habit surfaced most often after moments of cognitive overload rather than emotional distress, how it followed periods of intense focus, how it was preceded by subtle shifts in her internal dialogue.

One evening, as the familiar urge began to rise, something different happened. The AI did not tell her to stop. It simply introduced a pause—thirty seconds of guided attention that redirected her breathing and posture. The urge faltered. Confused, her brain hesitated, unsure whether to proceed. In that hesitation, the habit lost momentum. Sophia felt a strange sense of relief, not because she had resisted, but because the compulsion no longer felt inevitable.

Over the next few weeks, the system refined its timing. Sometimes it intervened with a pause, other times with an alternative action that offered a similar sense of release. Each successful interruption was acknowledged quietly, without praise or pressure. Sophia noticed that the habit no longer dominated her awareness. It began to feel optional rather than compulsory. The brain, deprived of its expected reward, gradually disengaged from the loop.

Months later, Sophia reflected on the change. She hadn't defeated the habit through force or shame. It had simply faded, replaced by behaviors that felt more aligned with who she was becoming. The AI hadn't controlled her choices; it had illuminated the moment where choice actually existed. By creating space between impulse and action, it allowed her brain to learn something new—that relief could come without retreat, that control could feel calm rather than tense.

Sophia realized then that the most powerful change had not been the disappearance of the habit, but the emergence of trust in her own agency. The pause had become her ally, a quiet signal that the brain was no longer trapped in repetition. With intelligence guiding adaptation rather than willpower enforcing restraint, her behavior transformed naturally, as if the brain had finally been given permission to choose differently.

Chapter 3

AI Therapy and the Reinforcement of Self-Control Networks

Self-control is often misunderstood as an internal battle between desire and discipline, but neuroscience reveals it as a function of specific neural networks responsible for regulation, foresight, and inhibition. These networks, primarily located in the prefrontal cortex, allow the brain to delay gratification, evaluate long-term consequences, and override automatic impulses generated by older subcortical systems. Self-control is not an unlimited resource; it is a trainable but fragile capacity that fluctuates based on stress, fatigue, emotional load, and environmental demands. Artificial intelligence reshapes the way self-control is developed by shifting the focus from forceful restraint to strategic neural reinforcement.

In the absence of adequate regulation, the brain defaults to efficiency. Automatic behaviors, habits, and emotional reactions require less cognitive energy than conscious decision-making. This is why stress reliably weakens self-control and why good intentions collapse under pressure. Traditional therapy often emphasizes insight and intention, yet insight alone does not strengthen regulatory circuits. AI therapy addresses this gap by focusing on repetition, timing, and reinforcement—the same principles that originally shaped automatic behavior. Instead of asking the brain to resist impulses indefinitely, AI systems train the brain to respond differently through gradual, adaptive conditioning.

AI-based therapeutic systems monitor the state of regulatory capacity in real time. By analyzing indicators such as cognitive workload, emotional volatility, sleep quality, and language complexity, AI can infer when self-control resources are depleted. During these moments, rather than demanding restraint, the system reduces decision complexity, introduces supportive scaffolding, or delays exposure to high-risk triggers. This protects regulatory networks from overload and prevents repeated failures that weaken confidence and neural resilience. Over time, this approach teaches the brain that regulation does not require exhaustion, fostering stability rather than strain.

Strengthening self-control networks requires repeated successful inhibition paired with meaningful reinforcement. AI systems create controlled opportunities for regulation by introducing manageable challenges calibrated to the individual's current capacity. When the brain successfully navigates these challenges, the system provides immediate feedback that reinforces the neural pathway associated with control. This feedback may take the form of progress reflection, cognitive reframing, or subtle reward cues that strengthen dopamine associations with regulation rather than impulsivity. The brain learns that restraint itself is rewarding, not merely restrictive.

AI therapy also reframes lapses in self-control as expected data rather than personal failures. When regulation breaks down, the system analyzes contributing variables rather than assigning blame. This analytical approach reduces emotional reactivity, which is itself a major disruptor of executive function. By removing shame from the equation, AI allows regulatory networks to recover more quickly and remain engaged. Over time, this reduces the volatility that often accompanies behavioral change efforts, stabilizing both emotional and cognitive control.

A key advantage of AI-driven self-control training is its ability to operate continuously rather than episodically. Human therapists typically engage clients in discrete sessions, limiting reinforcement opportunities. AI systems, however, embed therapeutic logic into daily life, offering micro-interventions that accumulate over time. These repeated exposures strengthen neural pathways incrementally, creating durable changes that persist even when external guidance is reduced. The brain adapts not because it is instructed to change, but because it is repeatedly rewarded for doing so. Self-control is also deeply linked to identity and self-trust. Repeated failures erode the brain's expectation of success, weakening motivation and increasing reliance on automatic behavior. AI therapy counteracts this by tracking and reinforcing consistency rather than perfection. Each successful act of regulation, no matter how small, is logged and reflected back to the individual as evidence of capability. This strengthens the brain's predictive model of itself, making future regulation more likely. Over time, self-control shifts from an effortful act to an expected outcome.

Ultimately, AI therapy reframes self-control as a learnable neural skill rather than a moral attribute. By aligning interventions with the brain's learning mechanisms, AI strengthens executive function in a sustainable way. This chapter establishes how AI systems reinforce regulatory networks, laying the groundwork for long-term behavioral stability. As self-control becomes neurologically embedded, individuals gain not just restraint, but confidence in their capacity to act in alignment with their values—even under pressure.

The Quiet Strength of Holding Back

Ethan had always prided himself on being driven. He worked long hours, set ambitious goals, and pushed himself relentlessly. Yet beneath that discipline lived a pattern he couldn't explain. When pressure peaked, his control vanished. He made impulsive decisions he later regretted, spoke words he wished he could retract, and sabotaged progress in moments of exhaustion. The harder he tried to stay in control, the faster it slipped away. He believed his problem was weakness, but what he didn't understand was that his regulatory systems were simply overworked.

When Ethan began using an AI-guided therapy platform, he expected strategies to "stay strong." Instead, the system focused on recovery. It tracked his sleep, his workload, and the subtle changes in his language as deadlines approached. It identified a consistent pattern: his lapses occurred not because he lacked discipline, but because his cognitive capacity had been depleted. The brain, exhausted, defaulted to speed over wisdom.

During a particularly demanding week, the system adjusted his environment without him realizing it. Notifications were reduced, decisions were simplified, and moments of rest were introduced strategically. When Ethan faced situations that usually triggered impulsive reactions, the AI offered brief pauses—not commands, but space. In those pauses, he noticed something unfamiliar: clarity. The urge to react lost its urgency.

Over time, the system increased the challenge gradually. Ethan began practicing restraint in small, controlled moments. Each success was acknowledged quietly, without celebration or pressure. The brain began to associate calm control with competence rather than sacrifice. Ethan felt less like he was fighting himself and more like he was working with his own limits.

Months later, Ethan reflected on how different he felt under stress. The impulses hadn't disappeared, but they no longer dictated his behavior. He trusted himself in ways he never had before. The AI hadn't made him disciplined; it had made him regulated. By protecting his cognitive resources and reinforcing success, it allowed his brain to build strength without breaking.

Ethan realized that true self-control was not loud or forceful. It was quiet, steady, and sustainable. And once the brain learned that holding back did not mean losing power, regulation became not a struggle, but a skill—one he carried with him long after the guidance faded.

Chapter 4

AI Coaching, Identity Reinforcement, and Lasting Behavioral Transformation

Behavior does not change in isolation; it changes in relationship to identity. The brain does not merely ask what action to take—it asks who is acting. Every repeated behavior reinforces an internal narrative about capability, character, and self-concept. When behavior conflicts with identity, the brain experiences cognitive friction and often defaults back to familiar patterns. This is why short-term behavior change is common while long-term transformation is rare. Artificial intelligence fundamentally alters this equation by aligning behavioral coaching with identity reinforcement, allowing change to stabilize at the deepest cognitive level.

Identity is encoded neurologically through networks that integrate memory, emotion, belief, and expectation. These networks influence decision-making long before conscious reasoning occurs. Traditional coaching often focuses on goals and actions without adequately addressing identity-level resistance. AI coaching systems operate differently. By analyzing language, choices, emotional tone, and consistency over time, AI builds a dynamic model of how an individual perceives themselves. This model allows the system to introduce behavioral challenges that align with emerging identity rather than conflict with it, reducing internal resistance and accelerating integration.

One of the most powerful aspects of AI coaching is its ability to detect identity drift in real time. Identity is not static; it fluctuates under stress, success, and social influence. When individuals revert to old behaviors, it is often because their internal identity narrative has regressed. AI systems recognize these shifts through changes in self-referential language, emotional framing, and decision latency. Instead of responding with correction or pressure, the system reinforces identity-consistent behaviors through reflection and evidence-based feedback. This stabilizes the self-concept and prevents regression before it manifests behaviorally.

AI coaching reframes success not as achievement, but as consistency. The brain learns identity through repetition, not peak performance. By tracking small, repeatable behaviors over time, AI systems reinforce the perception of reliability rather than intensity. This reduces the all-or-nothing thinking that undermines behavioral change efforts. When the brain expects consistency rather than perfection, it remains engaged even during setbacks. AI's impartial tracking and reflection help the individual internalize a new identity based on observable patterns rather than aspirational ideals. Another critical function of AI coaching is narrative restructuring. Humans interpret their lives through stories, and these stories shape behavior. AI systems analyze narrative patterns in journaling, speech, and reflection, identifying limiting beliefs and reinforcing adaptive narratives. When behavior shifts, the system mirrors these changes back to the individual in language that reinforces growth. This creates a feedback loop where behavior informs identity and identity supports behavior. Over time, the narrative of "trying to change" is replaced by the narrative of "this is who I am."

AI coaching also mitigates the destabilizing effects of external validation. Many behavioral change efforts fail because motivation depends on social reinforcement that is inconsistent or absent. AI systems provide stable, nonjudgmental feedback that does not fluctuate based on mood or circumstance. This allows the brain to anchor identity internally rather than externally. As self-trust increases, reliance on validation decreases, making behavioral change more resilient across environments and life transitions.

Importantly, AI does not impose identity—it reveals it. By highlighting patterns of strength, resilience, and capability already present in behavior, AI helps individuals recognize traits they may have overlooked. This recognition strengthens self-efficacy and increases willingness to engage in future challenges. The brain becomes more open to growth when it perceives change as an extension of self rather than a departure from it.

Sustainable transformation occurs when behavior, identity, and neural structure align. AI coaching facilitates this alignment by operating across all three layers simultaneously. It guides behavior, reinforces identity, and strengthens neural pathways through repetition and reward. The result is not forced change, but organic evolution. In this model, growth is not something to maintain through effort—it becomes the default expression of a newly integrated self.

Becoming the Person Who No Longer Has to Try

Lena had always described herself as "inconsistent." It was a word she used casually, almost affectionately, but it shaped everything she attempted. She would begin projects with enthusiasm, commit to routines with confidence, and then quietly abandon them weeks later. Each time reinforced the same conclusion: this was simply who she was. When she started using an AI coaching system, she expected productivity tips. What she encountered instead was reflection.

The system asked her to write short daily check-ins—not about goals, but about how she experienced herself that day. Over time, it noticed something Lena had never articulated. On days when she followed through, her language shifted subtly. She used fewer qualifiers, fewer apologies, fewer doubts. The system began reflecting this back to her, not as praise, but as observation. "You acted consistently today," it would note. "This aligns with the pattern you've been building."

At first, Lena resisted the idea. She felt like an imposter wearing a temporary mask of discipline. But the feedback continued, grounded in data rather than encouragement. Weeks passed. The system tracked her consistency across small behaviors—sleep routines, work blocks, moments of pause instead of avoidance. Slowly, the word "inconsistent" began to feel inaccurate. It no longer described her experience.

One afternoon, faced with a familiar choice between quitting and continuing, Lena noticed something unexpected. The decision didn't feel heavy. There was no internal debate, no motivational speech required. Continuing simply felt normal. The identity she had practiced—reinforced quietly, repeatedly—had taken hold. The behavior followed naturally.

Months later, Lena reflected on the change. She had not forced herself to become someone new. She had been shown who she already was becoming. The AI hadn't demanded transformation; it had documented it until the evidence was undeniable. Consistency was no longer something she chased.

It was something she trusted.

Lena realized then that the most powerful shift was not behavioral, but personal. She no longer asked whether she could maintain change. She assumed she would. And in that assumption, her brain found stability—not through effort, but through alignment with an identity that finally felt true.

Chapter 5

AI-Guided Addiction Recovery, Compulsion Extinction, and Relapse Prevention

Addiction is not a failure of character or a lack of motivation; it is a form of learned neuroplasticity that has become maladaptive. The brain, optimized for survival, forms powerful reinforcement loops around substances, behaviors, or stimuli that reliably alter emotional state or relieve discomfort. Over time, these loops dominate attention, motivation, and decision-making, reshaping neural priorities around immediate relief rather than long-term outcomes. Traditional addiction treatment often addresses behavior at the surface level, but artificial intelligence allows recovery to be approached as a process of neural retraining rather than behavioral suppression.

At the neurological level, addiction reflects an imbalance between reward circuitry and regulatory control systems. Dopamine pathways become hypersensitized, while prefrontal networks responsible for inhibition and foresight weaken through disuse. The brain learns to overvalue the addictive stimulus and undervalue alternative rewards. AI therapy systems model this imbalance with precision by tracking craving patterns, emotional triggers, environmental context, and physiological indicators. This continuous modeling allows addiction to be treated not as a static diagnosis, but as a dynamic state that fluctuates across time and circumstance.

One of the most dangerous aspects of addiction is its predictive nature. Cravings often emerge before conscious awareness, triggered by subtle cues such as stress, fatigue, loneliness, or environmental association. AI systems excel at detecting these early signals. By analyzing patterns across weeks and months, AI can identify the conditions that precede relapse with greater accuracy than self-report alone. This predictive capacity enables interventions to occur before craving escalates into compulsion, shifting recovery from reactive to proactive.

AI-guided recovery emphasizes extinction rather than suppression. Suppression relies on willpower, which is limited and easily depleted. Extinction, by contrast, weakens the neural association between cue and reward through repeated non-reinforcement. AI systems facilitate extinction by disrupting expected outcomes in a controlled and adaptive manner. When a cue appears, the system intervenes to prevent reward delivery while offering alternative regulatory strategies. Over time, the brain learns that the addictive behavior no longer produces its expected effect, reducing craving intensity and frequency. Relapse is traditionally viewed as failure, but from a neural perspective, it is feedback. AI reframes relapse as data that improves the behavioral model. When relapse occurs, the system analyzes contributing factors without judgment, identifying which variables overwhelmed regulatory capacity. This analysis allows future interventions to be adjusted, strengthening protective factors and reducing exposure to high-risk states. By removing shame from relapse, AI reduces emotional spirals that often prolong addictive cycles.

AI therapy also addresses the emotional and identity dimensions of addiction. Many individuals unconsciously identify with their addiction, using it to regulate emotion, manage stress, or define social belonging. AI coaching systems track narrative language and belief patterns, gradually reinforcing alternative identities that are incompatible with compulsive behavior. As individuals experience success in regulation and recovery, the system reflects these changes back as evidence of capability rather than abstinence alone. This identity reinforcement stabilizes recovery by aligning self-concept with health rather than struggle.

Long-term recovery depends on restoring balance to the brain's reward system. AI systems support this by helping individuals rediscover and reinforce non-addictive sources of reward. Through experimentation and feedback, the system identifies activities, relationships, and cognitive states that generate sustainable dopamine responses. Over time, these alternatives compete effectively with addictive stimuli, allowing the brain to recalibrate its reward hierarchy. Recovery becomes not a life of deprivation, but one of expanded engagement.

Perhaps most importantly, AI enables recovery to unfold gradually and privately. Many individuals avoid seeking help due to stigma or fear of judgment. AI systems provide confidential, nonjudgmental support that meets individuals where they are. This accessibility increases early intervention and reduces the severity of addiction before it escalates. By embedding recovery into daily life rather than isolating it within treatment settings, AI creates conditions for durable change.

Addiction recovery is not about erasing desire; it is about restoring choice. AI therapy strengthens the neural pathways that allow pause, reflection, and redirection. As regulatory networks recover and reward systems rebalance, the brain regains flexibility. Cravings lose their authority, and behavior becomes guided by values rather than compulsion. In this model, recovery is not a singular event, but a progressive realignment of neural systems toward stability, agency, and long-term well-being.

The Day the Urge Lost Its Voice

Marcus had lived with the urge for so long that he believed it was part of him. It arrived without warning, sometimes gentle, sometimes overwhelming, but always persuasive. He had learned to negotiate with it, delay it, promise himself moderation. None of it lasted. Each relapse felt less like a choice and more like gravity pulling him back to a familiar center. He told himself he lacked strength, unaware that his brain had simply learned too well.

When Marcus began using an AI-guided recovery system, he expected reminders to resist. Instead, the system focused on observation. It tracked his sleep, stress levels, work patterns, and emotional check-ins. It noticed that his strongest urges didn't appear during emotional lows, but during moments of relief—after deadlines, after social interactions, after long periods of control. The brain, anticipating reward, reached automatically for what it knew.

One evening, as the urge began to rise, the system intervened quietly. It didn't warn him or scold him. It offered a brief redirection—an activity designed to interrupt the reward expectation without demanding resistance. Marcus followed it half-heartedly, surprised by how quickly the craving softened. The urge didn't disappear, but it lost urgency. The brain, confused by the absence of reinforcement, hesitated.

Over the following weeks, these moments accumulated. Sometimes Marcus slipped, but the system responded with analysis rather than disappointment. It adjusted timing, increased support during vulnerable windows, and reinforced alternative rewards that actually resonated with him. Slowly, the cravings became less predictable, less commanding. They arrived as suggestions rather than orders.

Months later, Marcus experienced something unfamiliar. An urge surfaced—and passed. There was no negotiation, no internal battle. It simply faded, unsupported. Marcus realized then that the addiction had not been defeated through force. It had been outlearned. The brain had discovered new pathways, new sources of regulation, new expectations.

Marcus no longer defined himself by avoidance. He trusted his ability to choose. The AI hadn't removed desire; it had returned agency. And in that quiet restoration of choice, the urge lost its voice—not because it was silenced, but because it was no longer believed.

Chapter 6

AI-Assisted Long-Term Behavioral Maintenance and Emotional Resilience

Behavioral change is often treated as a destination rather than a process, yet the brain does not stabilize through achievement alone. It stabilizes through repetition, predictability, and emotional safety. Many individuals succeed in changing habits, overcoming addiction, or strengthening self-control, only to struggle months later when life circumstances shift. Stress, loss, success, aging, or environmental change can destabilize even well-established behavioral patterns. Artificial intelligence plays a critical role in long-term behavioral maintenance by adapting alongside the individual rather than assuming permanence once change has occurred.

The brain's capacity for regulation depends heavily on emotional resilience. Emotional resilience is not the absence of stress, but the ability to return to baseline efficiently after disruption. This capacity is governed by interactions between the autonomic nervous system, limbic structures, and executive control networks. When resilience is low, the brain becomes reactive, defaulting to familiar behaviors regardless of long-term goals. AI-assisted systems monitor resilience indicators continuously, identifying early signs of dysregulation before behavior deteriorates. This allows intervention at the level of nervous system stabilization rather than behavioral correction.

Long-term maintenance requires shifting from intervention-driven change to self-sustaining regulation. AI systems facilitate this transition by gradually reducing external prompts while reinforcing internal cues. Early in the change process, AI may provide frequent guidance. As stability increases, the system transitions into a background role, intervening only when risk indicators rise. This mirrors how the brain learns independence—through supported autonomy rather than abrupt withdrawal of structure. By matching support intensity to neural readiness, AI prevents both dependency and abandonment.

Life-stage transitions pose a unique challenge to behavioral stability. Changes in career, relationships, health, or aging alter cognitive load and emotional capacity. Behaviors that were once sustainable may become burdensome under new conditions. AI systems adapt to these transitions by recalibrating expectations and strategies based on real-time data. Instead of framing adaptation as regression, AI treats it as evolution. This preserves self-efficacy and prevents the identity collapse that often accompanies major life changes. Emotional resilience is strengthened through repeated exposure to manageable stress followed by successful recovery. AI systems support this process by tracking recovery time rather than stress intensity. The brain learns resilience not by avoiding challenge, but by experiencing its own capacity to recover. AI coaching highlights recovery success, reinforcing neural pathways associated with regulation and confidence. Over time, the brain becomes less reactive, more flexible, and more trusting of its own stability.

A critical component of long-term maintenance is emotional literacy. Many behavioral regressions occur because individuals misinterpret emotional signals as threats rather than information. AI systems analyze emotional patterns and help individuals contextualize their internal states. By normalizing fluctuations and identifying patterns, AI reduces catastrophizing and emotional amplification. This cognitive reframing preserves regulatory capacity and prevents stress from cascading into behavior relapse.

AI-assisted maintenance also addresses the accumulation of cognitive fatigue. Modern environments place constant demands on attention and decision-making, gradually eroding executive function. AI systems help manage this fatigue by optimizing routines, reducing unnecessary decisions, and encouraging restorative behaviors. These adjustments preserve self-control resources and extend the longevity of behavioral change. Maintenance becomes less about effort and more about intelligent energy allocation.

Ultimately, long-term behavioral stability emerges when the brain trusts its environment and its own regulatory capacity. AI contributes to this trust by providing consistency, predictability, and adaptive support. It does not freeze behavior in place, but allows it to evolve without collapse. In this model, change is not something to protect—it is something the brain learns to navigate with confidence. AI becomes a silent partner in resilience, ensuring that growth endures not because life remains stable, but because the individual becomes adaptable.

Learning to Stay Standing When the Ground Moves

Rachel thought the hardest part was over. She had rebuilt her habits, stabilized her emotions, and regained control over behaviors that once felt impossible to manage. For months, life felt steady. Then everything changed at once. A new job, a relocation, and the quiet weight of responsibility altered her routines overnight. The structure that had supported her growth disappeared, and with it came a familiar unease. She feared that all the progress had been temporary.

The AI system she had been using did not respond with urgency or alarm. Instead, it adjusted. It reduced expectations, simplified routines, and introduced small moments of regulation throughout her day. When Rachel felt overwhelmed, the system reflected back patterns she couldn't see—that her stress was situational, not personal, and that her recovery time was shortening even as demands increased. This perspective softened her self-judgment.

Some days were harder than others. Rachel noticed moments when old impulses resurfaced, not as cravings, but as invitations to escape. Each time, the system responded quietly, offering grounding rather than correction. It tracked not whether she struggled, but how quickly she recovered. Slowly, Rachel realized that she was not falling apart—she was adapting.

Weeks passed, and something shifted. The stressors remained, but her reaction to them changed. She no longer panicked at emotional fluctuations. She trusted her ability to stabilize. The habits she had built flexed rather than broke, reshaping themselves to fit her new reality. The AI, once more active, receded into the background.

One evening, reflecting on the transition, Rachel understood what had changed. Stability was no longer something she relied on externally. It lived within her nervous system. The AI had not preserved her old life—it had taught her how to remain regulated when life moved beneath her feet.

Rachel no longer feared change. She knew now that resilience was not rigidity, but responsiveness. And with that understanding, she stepped into the next phase of her life not guarded, but grounded—confident that whatever shifted next, she would remain standing.

Chapter 7

Ethical AI Therapy, Human Autonomy, and the Future of Behavioral Mastery

As artificial intelligence becomes more deeply integrated into therapy, coaching, and behavioral guidance, a fundamental question emerges: how do we ensure that intelligence enhances human autonomy rather than replacing it. Behavioral change is an intimate process, touching identity, emotion, belief, and vulnerability. Any system that operates in this space must be designed not only for effectiveness, but for ethical alignment with human agency. The future of AI-powered behavioral mastery depends not on how much control systems exert, but on how responsibly they amplify choice.

Ethical AI therapy begins with transparency. The human brain responds differently when it understands the nature of influence acting upon it. Hidden manipulation, even when well-intentioned, undermines trust and destabilizes self-regulation. AI systems designed for behavioral change must make their role explicit, allowing individuals to understand when guidance is being offered and why. This transparency preserves cognitive sovereignty, enabling the brain to integrate AI support as a tool rather than an authority.

When individuals perceive AI as collaborative rather than directive, resistance decreases and learning accelerates.

Autonomy is reinforced when AI systems prioritize consent-based intervention. Rather than imposing behavioral correction, ethical systems seek permission to engage at moments of vulnerability. This mirrors healthy human therapeutic relationships, where trust is built through respect rather than coercion. By allowing individuals to opt into guidance, AI reinforces the neural pathways associated with self-efficacy. The brain learns not that it is being controlled, but that it is choosing support. This distinction is critical for long-term behavioral stability.

Another ethical consideration lies in dependency prevention. While AI systems can provide continuous support, overreliance risks weakening internal regulatory capacity. Ethical AI coaching systems are designed to fade into the background as competence increases. They measure success not by engagement metrics, but by independence indicators—longer intervals without intervention, faster self-regulation, and sustained behavioral alignment without prompts. This gradual withdrawal mirrors effective education and therapy, ensuring that mastery belongs to the individual rather than the system.

Data stewardship is equally central to ethical AI therapy. Behavioral data is among the most sensitive forms of personal information, revealing emotional patterns, vulnerabilities, and identity markers. Ethical systems minimize data retention, anonymize patterns where possible, and prioritize user control over data usage. Trust in AI-guided behavioral change depends on the assurance that insight will not become exploitation. When the brain feels safe, learning deepens. When it feels surveilled, regulation collapses.

The future of behavioral mastery lies in collaboration between human insight and artificial intelligence. AI excels at pattern recognition, prediction, and consistency. Humans excel at meaning-making, value judgment, and moral reasoning. When these strengths are integrated rather than substituted, behavioral change becomes both effective and humane. AI handles the complexity of data; humans retain authority over values and direction. This balance preserves dignity while enhancing capability.

As AI systems evolve, they will increasingly support proactive behavioral design rather than reactive correction. Instead of intervening after dysregulation occurs, AI will help individuals architect environments, routines, and identities that naturally support alignment. Behavioral mastery will shift from constant effort to intelligent design. In this future, therapy becomes less about fixing what is broken and more about cultivating conditions for sustained well-being.

Ultimately, the goal of AI therapy and coaching is not perfection, but freedom. Freedom from compulsive patterns, from emotional volatility, from identities shaped by past limitation. Ethical AI does not define who a person should become. It creates space for the brain to choose differently, repeatedly, until new patterns feel natural. In this model, mastery is not control over oneself—it is trust in one's ability to adapt, recover, and align with intention over time.

This book concludes with a vision of behavioral change that is neither mechanical nor mystical, but intelligent and humane. Artificial intelligence, when designed ethically, becomes not a replacement for human growth, but a catalyst for it. The future of the AI-powered mind is not domination or dependence—it is partnership, where technology supports the most human capacities of all: awareness, choice, and transformation.

The Moment She Didn't Need the System Anymore

Elena remembered the early days clearly—the constant check-ins, the quiet guidance, the reassurance that arrived just before overwhelm took hold. The AI system had been a steady presence during the most unstable period of her life. It helped her recognize patterns, interrupt old behaviors, and rebuild a sense of control she had lost years earlier. For a long time, she believed she would always need it. Gradually, something changed. The system spoke less. Interventions became rarer, appearing only during moments of genuine strain. Elena began to notice that she was responding before the guidance arrived. She paused instinctively. She reframed without prompting. Emotional waves rose and fell without pulling her under. The brain, once reactive, now felt spacious.

One evening, after navigating a difficult conversation with calm clarity, Elena checked the system's dashboard. It noted her recovery time, her regulation, her consistency—but offered no instruction. Just observation. She realized then that the system had shifted roles. It was no longer guiding her. It was witnessing her.

Days turned into weeks. The AI faded further into the background. Elena still knew it was there, but she no longer reached for it reflexively. She trusted her internal signals. When challenges arose, she didn't panic or search for correction. She responded. The skills were no longer borrowed—they were embodied.

Eventually, the system prompted her with a question rather than advice. "Do you feel supported, or complete?" Elena smiled. The answer surprised her. She felt complete—not finished, not perfect, but capable. She chose to reduce the system's presence, not out of rejection, but out of readiness. Elena understood then what ethical support truly meant. The AI had not shaped her identity. It had protected her capacity to shape it herself. By stepping back at the right moment, it affirmed her autonomy rather than claiming credit for her growth.

As Elena moved forward, she carried the system not as a crutch, but as a chapter—one that had taught her how to listen to herself. The technology had done its job. The rest belonged to her.

Chapter 8

Designing a Self-Regulating Life with AI as a Background Intelligence

The ultimate goal of behavioral change is not continuous intervention, but self-regulation embedded so deeply into daily life that effort becomes unnecessary. Many approaches to behavior modification focus on fixing problems as they arise, creating an endless loop of correction and recovery. Artificial intelligence introduces a different paradigm: behavioral design. Rather than reacting to failure, AI helps individuals architect lives that naturally support alignment, reducing the need for constant self-control. In this model, behavior is not managed—it is guided by environment, structure, and identity working in harmony.

Self-regulation emerges most reliably when cognitive load is minimized and emotional safety is maximized. The brain performs best when it is not forced to constantly override impulses, but when impulses themselves are shaped by context. AI systems analyze daily routines, decision density, emotional fluctuations, and environmental triggers to identify friction points that undermine regulation. Instead of asking the individual to become stronger, AI redesigns the conditions that previously required strength. This shift from personal force to structural intelligence marks a fundamental evolution in behavioral mastery.

AI-assisted life design operates by aligning goals, energy, and environment. The brain's capacity for regulation varies across time, influenced by sleep, nutrition, stress, and social interaction. AI systems track these fluctuations and help schedule demanding activities during periods of peak capacity while protecting low-capacity windows from excessive demand. Over time, this alignment trains the brain to associate success with sustainability rather than strain. Behavior stabilizes not because the individual tries harder, but because the system supports natural rhythms.

Another critical aspect of self-regulating life design is anticipatory adaptation. Life rarely remains static, and many behavioral breakdowns occur not because of weakness, but because systems fail to adjust to new demands. AI systems excel at forecasting change by recognizing early indicators of transition—shifts in workload, emotional tone, routine disruption, or social context. By responding early, AI allows individuals to adjust expectations, routines, and goals before instability escalates. This proactive flexibility preserves behavioral integrity across seasons of life. AI also supports behavioral self-authorship by helping individuals define values-driven priorities. When behavior is guided by external pressure or vague ambition, regulation feels exhausting. AI coaching systems assist in clarifying values through pattern analysis, revealing which activities consistently produce satisfaction, engagement, and resilience. By highlighting these patterns, AI helps individuals commit to paths that are neurologically rewarding and emotionally sustainable. Behavior becomes an expression of identity rather than compliance with obligation.

Importantly, self-regulating systems must allow for imperfection. Rigid optimization leads to fragility, not mastery. AI life design emphasizes elasticity—structures that bend rather than break under pressure. By monitoring recovery rather than perfection, AI reinforces adaptability as a success metric. This reframing reduces fear of failure and prevents the stress cycles that often precipitate relapse. The brain learns that stability is maintained through responsiveness, not rigidity.

As AI transitions into a background intelligence, its presence becomes less directive and more supportive. The system operates quietly, intervening only when deviation threatens long-term alignment. This invisibility is not absence, but maturity. The individual no longer experiences AI as a guide, but as an underlying architecture that supports agency. Behavioral mastery, in this context, is indistinguishable from living well. Ultimately, designing a self-regulating life means moving beyond behavior change toward behavioral freedom. Freedom is not the absence of structure, but the presence of intelligent structure that removes unnecessary struggle. AI, when ethically and thoughtfully integrated, becomes a collaborator in this freedom. It does not dictate choices, but creates conditions in which the best choices emerge naturally. In doing so, it allows individuals to focus less on managing themselves and more on living with intention, creativity, and confidence.

When Life Finally Ran Smoothly

Jonah used to think adulthood was about managing chaos. Every day felt like a series of decisions demanding restraint—what to eat, how to respond, when to stop working, when to rest. He believed that if he ever relaxed, everything would unravel. The AI system he began using years earlier helped him stabilize, then grow, then adapt. Eventually, something unexpected happened. The struggle faded.

The system no longer interrupted Jonah's day with suggestions or corrections. Instead, it operated quietly, adjusting his environment and schedule in ways he barely noticed. Meetings shifted to times when his focus was sharpest. Rest appeared naturally after periods of intensity. Old triggers lost relevance because the contexts that produced them had disappeared. Jonah realized he wasn't exerting control anymore. He was simply moving through a life that fit him.

When unexpected stress arrived—a family issue, a work transition—Jonah braced for regression. But it never came. The system adjusted in advance, lightening cognitive load and reminding him of recovery patterns that had worked before. Jonah didn't feel heroic. He felt steady. The behaviors he once worked tirelessly to maintain now required no effort at all.

One afternoon, sitting in a quiet café, Jonah noticed something subtle. He wasn't monitoring himself. He wasn't scanning for danger or temptation. He was present. The AI had done what no motivational system ever had—it had removed itself from the foreground of his life. He felt free, not because there were no constraints, but because the constraints were intelligent.

Jonah understood then that mastery was not about discipline. It was about design. The system hadn't made him stronger; it had made life easier to navigate. By aligning his environment, energy, and values, it allowed his best behavior to become automatic.

As Jonah closed his notebook and stepped back into his day, he carried no sense of vigilance—only trust. Trust that his life was structured to support him, trust that adaptation would come when needed, and trust that he no longer had to manage himself to live well. The intelligence was there, quietly ensuring that the path ahead remained smooth.

Chapter 9

Behavioral Longevity, Aging Minds, and Long-Horizon Self-Governance with AI

Behavioral mastery is often framed within short timelines—breaking a habit, achieving stability, completing recovery—but the true challenge lies in sustaining agency across decades. As the brain ages, cognitive resources shift, emotional processing evolves, and priorities realign. Behavioral systems that function well in early adulthood may become inefficient or even counterproductive later in life. Artificial intelligence offers a framework for behavioral longevity by supporting adaptation across the lifespan rather than locking individuals into static models of success.

Aging is not a linear decline, but a redistribution of cognitive strengths. While processing speed may slow, pattern recognition, emotional intelligence, and integrative reasoning often improve. Behavioral instability arises when systems fail to account for these changes, demanding performance from capacities that are naturally transitioning. AI-assisted behavioral governance recognizes these shifts by continuously updating its understanding of cognitive capacity, emotional resilience, and recovery time. This allows behavioral expectations to evolve without compromising self-efficacy or identity.

Long-horizon decision-making becomes increasingly important as time perspective expands. Choices made in midlife and beyond carry compounded consequences for health, relationships, and meaning. AI systems support this expanded horizon by modeling long-term outcomes rather than immediate rewards. By visualizing future trajectories and reinforcing behaviors that align with extended well-being, AI helps the brain prioritize sustainability over urgency. This reframes decision-making from reactive optimization to generational stewardship of one's own life.

Behavioral longevity also depends on preserving curiosity and flexibility. Rigidity is one of the most common contributors to late-life dissatisfaction and behavioral decline. AI systems counteract rigidity by encouraging gentle experimentation and novelty calibrated to tolerance. The brain remains plastic when it feels safe to explore without risk of failure. By framing adaptation as learning rather than loss, AI sustains engagement with life even as circumstances change.

Emotional regulation across aging involves integrating experience rather than suppressing emotion. Older brains often process emotion more deeply, but may struggle with rapid environmental change. AI-assisted systems help manage this by smoothing transitions and reducing unnecessary cognitive strain. By tracking emotional recovery rather than emotional intensity, AI reinforces resilience and confidence in regulation. This preserves agency during periods of uncertainty, loss, or transformation.

Another critical dimension of behavioral longevity is legacy alignment. As individuals age, motivation increasingly shifts from achievement to contribution. AI coaching systems identify behaviors that support mentorship, creativity, and generativity. By aligning daily actions with a sense of purpose beyond the self, AI strengthens psychological well-being and reduces existential anxiety. Behavior becomes less about control and more about continuity.

Importantly, AI does not define what a meaningful life should look like at any stage. Instead, it helps individuals articulate their own evolving values and design behavior accordingly. This respects the uniqueness of each life trajectory while providing structural support for adaptation. Behavioral longevity is not about preserving youth, but about maintaining agency, dignity, and responsiveness as identity evolves.

In this context, AI becomes a long-term partner in self-governance. It does not aim to optimize every decision, but to preserve the capacity to choose well over time. By adjusting support to cognitive, emotional, and motivational shifts, AI ensures that behavioral mastery does not peak early and erode later. Instead, it becomes a lifelong practice—one that deepens rather than diminishes with age.

The Long View

Samuel had lived many versions of himself. There was the ambitious young man who chased milestones relentlessly, the steady builder who valued consistency, and the reflective thinker who began to care less about speed and more about direction. What surprised him most was not how much he had changed, but how often his systems lagged behind his identity. The habits that once served him well now felt heavy, as if they belonged to someone else.

The AI system Samuel used had been with him for years, evolving quietly in the background. It noticed shifts before he articulated them—how his decisions slowed, how his emotional responses deepened, how his priorities subtly reoriented toward meaning rather than momentum. Instead of pushing him to maintain past performance, the system adapted. It reduced urgency, increased space, and highlighted behaviors that aligned with his emerging values.

When Samuel faced decisions about health, work, and relationships, the system framed them in longer horizons. It showed him not just what would feel good now, but what would feel right years from now. This perspective calmed him. He stopped feeling behind and started feeling aligned. The pressure to optimize faded, replaced by a sense of stewardship over his remaining time.

One afternoon, walking through a park, Samuel reflected on how differently he experienced effort. He no longer measured success by intensity or volume. He measured it by continuity—how smoothly one season of life flowed into the next. The AI didn't tell him who to be. It helped him listen to who he was becoming.

As years passed, Samuel noticed something quietly profound. He trusted himself more, not less. Even as certain abilities softened, his confidence in navigating change strengthened. The system intervened rarely now, offering perspective rather than guidance. Samuel felt neither managed nor monitored. He felt accompanied.

Looking back, Samuel realized that the greatest gift of the intelligence he had partnered with was not efficiency or control. It was continuity. His life no longer felt like a series of disconnected phases, but a coherent arc. Behavior, identity, and values evolved together, supported by a system that respected time as an ally rather than an enemy. In that realization, Samuel found peace—not because everything was optimized, but because nothing essential was being rushed. The long view had finally come into focus, and with it, a calm assurance that he could continue choosing well, no matter how many chapters remained.

Chapter 10

Behavioral Sovereignty and the Future of Human–AI Co-Evolution

The ultimate measure of successful behavioral change is not compliance, optimization, or even consistency—it is sovereignty. Behavioral sovereignty refers to the sustained ability to govern one's actions, emotions, and identity over time without coercion, dependency, or loss of agency. As artificial intelligence becomes increasingly capable of guiding human behavior, the central question shifts from what AI can do to how humans remain authors of their own lives. This final chapter explores how behavioral mastery evolves into sovereignty and how human–AI co-evolution must be designed to preserve freedom rather than replace it.

Human behavior has always been shaped by tools. Language, culture, education, and technology have each influenced how the brain learns, adapts, and decides. AI represents the most intimate tool yet, operating not on the environment alone, but on cognition itself. When designed responsibly, AI does not override human choice—it sharpens it. Behavioral sovereignty emerges when AI enhances awareness without dictating outcomes, allowing individuals to perceive options more clearly while retaining the authority to choose among them.

Co-evolution implies mutual adaptation. As humans change with the aid of AI, AI systems must also evolve in response to human values, boundaries, and developmental readiness. Static systems risk either obsolescence or overreach. Adaptive systems, by contrast, adjust their role over time—from active guidance to quiet support to eventual dormancy. This lifecycle mirrors healthy mentorship, where guidance recedes as competence matures. Behavioral sovereignty is preserved when AI knows not only how to intervene, but when to step back.

A critical risk in advanced behavioral systems is subtle dependency. When decision-making becomes consistently mediated by external intelligence, internal regulatory capacity can atrophy. Ethical AI design counters this risk by prioritizing skill transfer over task completion. Each interaction should leave the individual more capable than before. Over time, AI's value shifts from solving problems to reinforcing the individual's confidence in solving them independently. Sovereignty grows when capability replaces reliance.

Behavioral mastery also requires tolerance for ambiguity. No system—human or artificial—can predict every future condition. Attempts to eliminate uncertainty often produce rigidity rather than resilience. AI systems that respect sovereignty do not aim to perfect behavior, but to prepare individuals to navigate uncertainty with composure. This preparation involves strengthening meta-skills: awareness, adaptability, emotional regulation, and reflective judgment. These capacities endure even when external support fades.

As AI becomes more integrated into society, behavioral sovereignty will increasingly define mental health, leadership, and fulfillment. Individuals who can collaborate with intelligent systems without surrendering autonomy will thrive in complex environments. Those who outsource identity, values, or judgment risk becoming optimized yet unanchored. This distinction underscores the importance of intentional design—not only of AI systems, but of one's relationship with them.

The future of human–AI co-evolution is not one of dominance or submission, but partnership. AI offers scale, consistency, and insight; humans provide meaning, ethics, and direction. When these roles remain distinct yet complementary, behavioral mastery deepens rather than diminishes humanity. The most advanced systems will not seek to shape human behavior toward predefined outcomes, but to support individuals in clarifying and living their own values across time.

This book has traced a progression—from rewiring habits, to restoring control, to designing sustainable lives, to preserving agency across decades. The destination is not perfection, but authorship. Behavioral sovereignty means that growth remains self-directed, resilient, and aligned even as tools grow more powerful. Artificial intelligence, at its best, becomes invisible not because it is absent, but because its purpose has been fulfilled.

In this final vision, AI does not define who we become. It protects our ability to choose who we are becoming. Behavioral mastery matures into sovereignty when intelligence supports freedom rather than replacing it. That is the future worth designing—one where technology amplifies the most human capacity of all: the ability to live deliberately.

The Choice That Was Finally His

Evan remembered when guidance had felt essential. There was a time when every decision required scaffolding, when the AI system beside him felt like a lifeline. It helped him regulate emotions, interrupt old patterns, and rebuild trust in himself. For years, the partnership had been active, visible, and necessary. What surprised him now was how quiet it had become.

One morning, Evan faced a decision that would once have triggered analysis, prompts, and reassurance. He noticed the absence immediately. No suggestion arrived. No framing appeared. The system was silent. For a moment, uncertainty flickered. Then something steadier replaced it—clarity. He paused, reflected, and chose. The decision felt neither impulsive nor optimized. It felt owned.

Later that day, Evan reviewed the system's activity log. It noted his choice, his emotional stability, and his recovery time. No feedback followed. Just acknowledgment. Evan understood then that the system was no longer guiding him because it no longer needed to. The skills had transferred. The agency had returned fully.

In the weeks that followed, Evan noticed a shift in how he related to challenge. He didn't look outward for correction. He looked inward for alignment. When uncertainty arose, it felt navigable rather than threatening. The intelligence that once lived outside him now felt internalized—not as code, but as confidence.

Eventually, Evan chose to archive the system. Not delete it, not reject it, but close the chapter with intention. The system responded with a single message, free of sentiment or instruction. It reflected his journey, his growth, and his readiness. Evan smiled. It was not a goodbye. It was a graduation.

Walking forward, Evan felt something rare—freedom without fragility. He knew he could return to support if needed, but he no longer feared navigating alone. The partnership had done what it was meant to do. It had not made him dependent. It had made him sovereign.

As Evan stepped into the next season of his life, he carried no instructions—only trust. Trust in his ability to adapt, to choose, and to grow without being managed. The intelligence had fulfilled its purpose, and what remained was unmistakably human: agency, authorship, and the quiet confidence of someone finally steering their own course.

Epilogue

From Behavioral Change to Nervous System Intelligence

Behavioral change, when examined closely, is never only about behavior. It is about regulation. Every habit, impulse, emotional reaction, and decision ultimately traces back to the state of the nervous system. A regulated system supports flexibility, reflection, and choice. A dysregulated system defaults to survival patterns—compulsion, avoidance, rigidity, and reactivity. Throughout this book, the role of artificial intelligence has been explored as a catalyst for rewiring behavior, strengthening self-control, and restoring agency. At its deepest level, however, AI's most powerful contribution is its capacity to support nervous system intelligence.

The nervous system governs the boundary between intention and action. When it is overwhelmed, even the most refined behavioral strategies collapse. When it is stable, change feels natural rather than forced. AI therapy and coaching succeed not because they impose structure, but because they sense, respond to, and stabilize internal states in real time. This is the hidden throughline connecting habit change, addiction recovery, identity reinforcement, and long-term resilience. AI works because it operates at the same speed as dysregulation, intervening before stress becomes behavior. As this book has demonstrated, sustainable change emerges when the brain no longer perceives threat in growth. Fear—of failure, loss, instability, or effort—activates defensive circuits that undermine learning. AI systems reduce this threat by creating predictability, timing interventions precisely, and adapting expectations dynamically. Over time, the nervous system learns that change does not equal danger. This learning is foundational. Without it, behavioral techniques remain fragile. With it, transformation becomes durable.

The transition from behavior modification to nervous system intelligence marks a shift from management to embodiment. Early stages of change require external scaffolding—guidance, feedback, interruption. As regulation improves, these supports recede, and internal signals become reliable. The individual no longer monitors behavior constantly; they feel aligned. AI's role evolves accordingly, moving from active guide to quiet stabilizer to optional companion. This progression is not accidental—it is essential for autonomy.

Crucially, nervous system intelligence is not static. It must adapt across environments, relationships, aging, and uncertainty. AI supports this adaptability by tracking recovery rather than perfection, resilience rather than resistance. When setbacks occur, the system responds with recalibration instead of correction. This prevents the shame and overexertion that destabilize regulation. The nervous system learns that fluctuation is normal and manageable, preserving trust in one's capacity to recover.

This book has emphasized that the future of AI therapy is not clinical dominance or algorithmic authority. It is partnership. A partnership in which AI respects biological rhythms, emotional limits, and human values. A partnership that strengthens internal capacity rather than replacing it. Behavioral change that bypasses the nervous system is temporary. Behavioral change that trains the nervous system becomes identity.

As you close this volume, it is important to recognize that behavior does not exist in isolation from rest, sleep, stress, and recovery. Regulation must be replenished. The same intelligence that rewires habits must also restore calm. This is where the journey continues. Book 6 expands the lens from behavioral mastery to physiological restoration, exploring how AI supports sleep quality, stress reduction, autonomic balance, and long-term healing. Together, these systems form a complete architecture of human adaptation.

Behavioral sovereignty is not achieved through constant effort. It is achieved when the nervous system feels safe enough to choose freely. AI, at its best, creates that safety—not by controlling outcomes, but by stabilizing the internal environment in which choice becomes possible. That is the lasting contribution of AI therapy and coaching: not behavior that must be maintained, but regulation that sustains itself.

This is not the end of the work. It is the point at which effort gives way to intelligence, and intelligence gives way to ease.

The Calm That Made Everything Possible

There was a time when Maya believed progress meant tension. Every improvement in her life had been accompanied by strain—tight schedules, relentless focus, constant self-monitoring. Even when she succeeded, her body never rested. The AI system she began using years earlier helped her change behaviors, interrupt patterns, and regain control, but something remained unsettled beneath the surface. She was functioning, but not calm.

Gradually, the system shifted its focus. Instead of tracking outcomes, it began tracking recovery. It noticed how long it took Maya to return to baseline after stress, how her breathing changed during decision-making, how sleep quality influenced her emotional range. Interventions became gentler. Less about doing, more about stabilizing. At first, Maya resisted. Calm felt unproductive. Then something unexpected happened. The calmer she became, the easier everything else felt. Decisions required less effort. Habits held without vigilance. Emotional waves passed without pulling her under. The behaviors she once worked tirelessly to maintain now emerged naturally. The nervous system, finally supported, no longer sabotaged her intentions.

One evening, after a long day that would once have left her exhausted and reactive, Maya noticed she felt steady. Not numb. Not detached. Just regulated. She realized then that nothing in her life had changed externally. What had changed was the internal environment in which everything occurred.

The AI system, once central, now sat quietly in the background. It intervened rarely, offering subtle reminders to rest, breathe, or pause when necessary. Maya trusted herself again—not because she was controlling herself, but because she felt safe inside her own body.

As she prepared for sleep that night, Maya reflected on the journey. Behavioral change had been the doorway, but regulation was the destination. The intelligence she had partnered with did not push her forward. It held her steady long enough for her to move freely on her own.

In that calm, Maya understood something profound. The life she wanted had never required more effort. It required a nervous system that no longer believed it was under threat.

With that foundation restored, everything else followed—quietly, naturally, and without force.

www.ingramcontent.com/pod-product-compliance
Ingram Content Group UK Ltd.
Pitfield, Milton Keynes, MK11 3LW, UK
UKHW020156290926
15471UKWH00005B/899

9 798295 627323